The Power of Simplicity – Lessons from Mother Nature

Meditative Haiku for inner peace

Dr. Samir Parag Heble

Copyright © 2019 by Dr. Samir Parag Heble. 732946
Library of Congress Control Number: 2019910721

ISBN: Softcover 978-1-7960-0512-7
Hardcover 978-1-7960-0511-0
EBook 978-1-7960-0513-4

All rights reserved. No part of this book may be reproduced or transmitted in any form or by any means, electronic or mechanical, including photocopying, recording, or by any information storage and retrieval system, without permission in writing from the copyright owner.

Print information available on the last page

Rev. date: 08/01/2019

To order additional copies of this book, contact:
Xlibris
1-800-455-039
www.xlibris.com.au
Orders@Xlibris.com.au

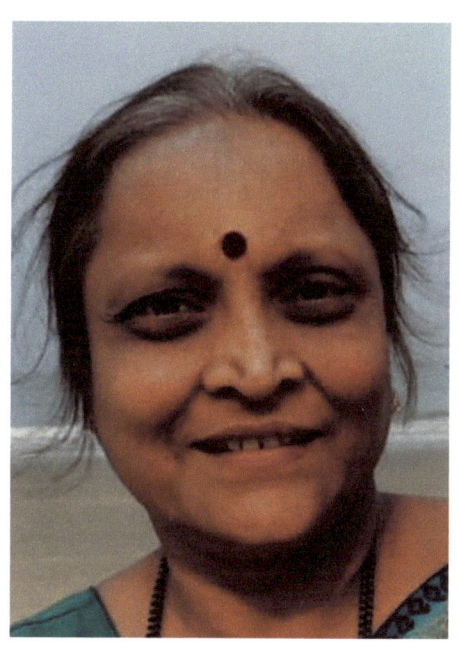

To my very dear mother-in-law Sulabha.

Sulabha taught me the grand power of simplicity and the essence of true spirituality. In her every breath , she taught us how to share our inherent goodness and God and showed us how to make this world more peaceful and beautiful.

Contents

Affirmation (Brahma Kumaris) vii
Introduction ix
Count Your Treasures 1
Reflection 5
Letting Go 9
Where Am I going? 13
The Grandeur of the Universe 17
My Mentors 21
I'm Never Alone 25
Order and Balance 29
Stillness 33
Nurturing with Care 37
Strength 41
Spices of Life 45
Rejuvenation 49
Power of Silence 53
Life Is an Adventure 57
Time to Pause 61
My God 65
Our Connection with Trees 69
Hidden Treasures 73

Simple Eating 77

Miracles of Life 81

Love 85

Every Day Is a Grand Day 89

Spreading Love 93

The Cycle of Life 97

In Search of Peace 101

Be a Child Again 105

Weathering the Storms 109

The Road Less Travelled 113

Getting to Your Feast 117

Welcome in All Guests 121

Finding the Sacred in Nature 125

The Pleasures of Giving 129

Colours of Life 133

Be an Early Bird 137

There's Always a Time for Everything 141

Cultivating Patience 145

Collaboration 149

Creativity 153

It's my mind.
I am the Master.
I choose which thought to create.
I decide for how long to think.
I choose which thought to hold on to.
And I choose which thought to let go.

-A Brahma Kumaris affirmation

Introduction

A haiku is a short Japanese verse of three lines used to evoke images and create self-awareness. Line one has five syllables, line two has seven, and line three has five.

This book is an example of modified meditative haiku written by me through my observations of nature and insights and learnings gained by me on this grand adventure and journey of life.

My best moments in life have been moments of silence . These serene moments have helped me gain new insights and cultivate wisdom. Each section has a blank page ('silence') which will help you work through the new insights that you may discover and rediscover.

I have found haiku poetry a useful tool in working with anxiety, depression, and other psychological disorders, as well as understanding better my own self and the beautiful universe around me. The words are simple yet profound. And every time I read them, I get new insights too. Enjoy!

Evening waves dancing
Setting sun kisses goodbye
I count my treasures

Lessons from Mother Nature

1. Look outside your window or in nature and count any three treasures out there.

___

2. Make a list of your treasures and write them in your special diary. See this list grow every day.

___

The cool silky beach
Invites me with open arms
Silence – reflection

Lessons from Mother Nature

1. *Keep some time in your day for silent reflection. Often the best insights can be gained from your moments of silence.*

   _____
   _____
   _____
   _____
   _____
   _____
   _____
   _____

2. *Consider keeping a place in your home to cultivate this practice of silent reflection.*

   _____
   _____
   _____
   _____
   _____
   _____
   _____
   _____
   _____

Leaves fall without fuss
Along the calm lakeside park
What should I let go?

Lessons from Mother Nature

1. Do you think you may be carrying too much baggage? Is there anything you need to let go to make your travels lighter?

_____
_____
_____
_____
_____
_____
_____
_____
_____
_____

As I climb these steps

I begin to ask myself

Where am I going?

Lessons from Mother Nature

Reflection time:

Where am I now, and where am I going?

*I stare at the skies
And the vastness of the seas
Universe is grand*

Lessons from Mother Nature

Did you know?

- -The universe is constantly expanding.

- -The Earth is around 4.5 billion years old, and our universe is three times its age

- -There are probably more than 170 billion galaxies in the observable universe.

- -There may be an infinite number of universes.

- -The human brain is the most complex object in the known universe with a hundred billion or more neurons and a quadrillion connections.

The lighthouse protects
From dangers far and beyond
I salute my guides

Lessons from Mother Nature

Reflection time:

Reflect on some of your teachers, mentors, supervisors, or guides who have brought you to the place where you are now. What did you learn from them? Send them meditatively your gratefulness thoughts.

_____
_____
_____
_____
_____
_____
_____
_____
_____
_____
_____
_____
_____
_____
_____
_____
_____
_____
_____
_____

No one is alone
Mother Earth embraces you
on your every path

Reflection time:

Loneliness empowers you with the beauty to discover your true self. It is when you discover your true self that you are in the midst of the universe. You begin to realise the truth that we are connected to everyone and everything. We are never alone.

Order and balance
Are crucial to existence
Peace be within all

Lessons from Mother Nature

Reflection time:

Our world has several facets: the biological, psychological, social, cultural, and spiritual dimensions. These are closely intertwined and in synch with one another. When these elements are in harmony with one another, we begin to experience inner peace.

Is there or are there any dimensions that you feel you need to give more time to experience your whole self?

_____
_____
_____
_____
_____
_____
_____
_____
_____
_____
_____
_____
_____
_____
_____

When the lake is still

The reflection is clear

Clear your mind now

Lessons from Mother Nature

Reflection time:

We tend to give a lot of time to look after our physical body: we wash ourselves regularly, go for walks, play a sport, go to the gym, use weights, etc. We 'clean' our physical body in many ways.

How often do we 'clean' our mind?

_____
_____
_____
_____
_____
_____
_____
_____
_____
_____
_____
_____
_____
_____
_____
_____
_____

Yellow chillies grow

In my pot nurtured with care

Wonderful feeling

I once met a lovely lady who said to me that whenever she feels down, she spends time in her garden. This is one of her 'self-soothing' strategies. She spends time with her plants that she calls her 'children'. She sows new seeds, and it gives her a sense of accomplishment, creation, and joy. She is in rhythm with nature, 'the best antidepressant'.

Make a list of your self-soothing strategies.

_____
_____
_____
_____
_____
_____
_____
_____
_____
_____
_____
_____
_____
_____

The pure lotus
Risen from harsh, muddy lands
Reminds me of strength

Lessons from Mother Nature

Did you know:

- The lotus flower grows in muddy water and rises above the surface to bloom with astounding beauty.

- The lotus symbolises the purity of the heart and the mind.

- It is the national flower of India, Egypt, and Vietnam.

- The lotus can adapt easily to any situation, whilst simultaneously purifying the water wherever it grows.

- In Buddhism, the lotus also represents 'transmigration'. The flower represents the past, the lotus shape represents the present, and the buds represent the future.

- It represents also refinement, mystery, contemplation, and the cleanliness of the soul despite its earthly surroundings.

- The lotus has been an ever-present inspiration for art, literature, food, and architecture.

Red, pungent chillies
They are so special to me
Spicing up my life

Lessons from Mother Nature

Reflection time:

For food to be tasty, it needs a combination of ingredients, all in the right amount and flavour – salt, sugar, herbs, spices, and chillies.

And so is life, it needs the 'chillies' and the spices as much as it needs the 'sugars' and the sweets.

_____
_____
_____
_____
_____
_____
_____
_____
_____
_____
_____
_____
_____

Create energies
Like the windmills on the hills
Rejuvenation

Did you know:

- *How wind turbines work: The energy in the wind turns two or three propeller-like blades around a rotor. The rotor is connected to the main shaft, which spins a generator to create electricity.*

- *Centuries ago, windmills were used to mill grain or pump water*

Are there any 'energies' within you or around you that you can harness and develop further?

_____
_____
_____
_____
_____
_____
_____
_____
_____
_____
_____

Giant karri trees
A mesmerising silence
Nature is sacred

Lessons from Mother Nature

Reflection time:

I am always awestruck when in the midst of greenery and forests. They help me rejuvenate, reboot myself, and reinvigorate.

The yellow canoes
On the grand Beedelup lake
Life's an adventure

Reflection time:

Life has taken me on a grand adventure: I was born in the idyllic city of Panjim in Goa, India, and was privileged to be taught by the Salesian Brothers and Fathers of Don Bosco school. At the age of twelve, I was introduced to the French culture and civilisation and got to travel across Europe. My thirties took me to the beautiful Taranaki region of New Plymouth, New Zealand, where we lived for ten years. For us, New Zealand was like a big beautiful garden. Australia welcomed us in my forties. The adventure continues to be awesome with all its rides, bumps, and thrills.

The rustic wood bench
Invites me to sit and pause
And take a deep breath

Lessons from Mother Nature

Reflection time:

'Breathe in calm, breathe out peace', a simple yet profound mantra that you can say three to five times a day, each time with three repetitions with inbreaths and outbreaths. See the difference it will make.

A monastery
Adorns the top of steep cliffs
My temple is me

Lessons from Mother Nature

Did you know:

- There are around 4,300 plus religions in the world

- Mahatma Gandhi referred to 'God' as 'Truth'. His mission was not only to humanise religion but also to moralise it. His interpretation of Hinduism, Islam, and Christianity made his religion a federation of different religious faiths.

For me, my 'God' is thinking good, speaking good, and doing and sharing good.

Take some time to write about your 'God' (or what the word means for you).

_____
_____
_____
_____
_____
_____
_____
_____
_____

Our bond is special
We exchange our precious breaths
I will protect you

Lessons from Mother Nature

Reflection time:

Trees are precious. Trees are special. Do you think we look after tress well enough? What can we do better?

_____
_____
_____
_____
_____
_____
_____
_____
_____
_____
_____
_____
_____
_____
_____
_____
_____

*When you look with care
You find hidden treasures
Magic is out there*

Lessons from Mother Nature

Reflection time:

Can you spot the luxury yacht in between the leaves? If you look carefully, you will see.

Life is full of treasures, often at our doorstep or in our own back yard. We just need to look with care.

_____
_____
_____
_____
_____
_____
_____
_____
_____
_____
_____
_____
_____
_____
_____

Lentil rice, lemon
Eating simple and healthy
Simple is the best

Lessons from Mother Nature

Did you know?

- Lentils are high in fibre and complex carbohydrates and low in fat and calories. They have high protein content.

- Lentils help lower blood cholesterol, blood sugars, and high blood pressure and protect against developing colon cancer.

- Lentils contain high folate that helps blood cells and nerves and protects against anaemia, heart disease, cancer, and dementia.

- Lentils Contain a good amount of iron and manganese.

Pollinating bees
Outside my bedroom window
Life's a miracle

Reflection time:

Every blade of grass is different, every piece of stone is different, the sky is grand every day, and the sunset is magical every time. These are just a few of the miracles of life.

A single red rose
Yet, the greatest gift of love
Less is often best

Lessons from Mother Nature

Reflection time:

What are some of the best gifts you have had or would like?

Early morning swim
Fills me up with energy
Another grand day

Lessons from Mother Nature

Reflection time:

Make a list of all the nice things that occur in your life every day. Read this list each night just before sleep. See this list grow every night.

_____

_____

_____

_____

_____

_____

_____

_____

_____

_____

_____

_____

_____

_____

_____

The sun has risen
The pink hibiscus has bloomed
Bee spreads seeds of love

Lessons from Mother Nature

Reflection time:

The bee and the flower have a symbiotic relationship. The flower gives the bee its rich nectar, and the bee, in turn, helps the plant reproduce through pollination. Is there a symbiotic relationship you have with anybody or the universe?

_____
_____
_____
_____
_____
_____
_____
_____
_____
_____
_____
_____
_____

*I watch the sun set
And reflect on my existence
Birth, growth, change and death*

Lessons from Mother Nature

Reflection time:

Reflect on one or more of these stages at your own pace. Thank the millions of beings and non-beings who have been a part of your life on this grand journey.

Deep in the forest
I am drawn to its silence
The peace is sublime

Reflection time:

Peace can be found internally as well as externally, both within you and around you. The forest is one such place, one of profound peace.

What are some of these special places of yours where you find peace?

_____
_____
_____
_____
_____
_____
_____
_____
_____
_____
_____
_____
_____
_____
_____

Ocean waves playing
Relaxing and refreshing
Be a child again

Lessons from Mother Nature

Reflection time:

Make a list of all your hobbies, your interests, what you are really passionate about. If you were a child again one day, which of these things would you like to revel in?

_____
_____
_____
_____
_____
_____
_____
_____
_____
_____
_____
_____
_____

The winds were quite strong
Yet, every leaf clung so tight
To weather the storm

Lessons from Mother Nature

Reflection time:

What are the various ways you may wish to look after yourself during a 'storm'?

The road less travelled
It's always an adventure
Fun, charm, and magic

Lessons from Mother Nature

Reflection time:

Jawaharlal Nehru once said, "Success comes to those who risk and dare". Have there been times when you went on a path that people don't usually take and came across something really interesting in your life?

_____
_____
_____
_____
_____
_____
_____
_____
_____
_____
_____
_____
_____
_____
_____
_____

It's begun to rain
The snail's up on the tree branch
It gets a rich feast

Lessons from Mother Nature

Did you know?

- Snails climb the bark of trees and feed on lichens, moss, and algae during times of high humidity, such as rain, dense fogs, humid nights, or in the mists found in higher elevation forests.

The bell at my door
Welcome all guests entering
All come for reason

Lessons from Mother Nature

Reflection time:

Our mind is like a guest house. Every moment, we have different guests entering in. Some of them are our 'wanted' guests (money, joy, rewards, fame, etc.), and some are our 'unwanted' or 'lesser wanted' guests (losses, anger, disappointments, etc.). We tend to open the door to the wanted guests but not to the unwanted guests. The more we close the door of our guest house to the unwanted guests, the more they keep on knocking. And therein lies the suffering. Inner bliss lies in acknowledging all guests (sometimes at your own pace) and over time accepting all guests. They all come in for a reason.

Even desert sands
Can nurture beautiful blooms
Search and you will find

Lessons from Mother Nature

Reflection time:

Have there been periods in your life when you found treasures in places you least expected?

_____
_____
_____
_____
_____
_____
_____
_____
_____
_____
_____
_____
_____
_____
_____
_____
_____

Delicate mangroves
Nurturing ecosystems
What am I giving?

Lessons from Mother Nature

Did you know:

Bunbury mangroves, Western Australia:

- The mangroves are an important part of the food chain in the waters of the Leschenault inlet in Bunbury. The trees help support sixty species of birds and numerous types of invertebrates that live in the saltmarsh and mudflats of Mangrove Cove.

- The mangrove leaves fall into water and are broken down by fungi. Fragments are eaten by fish and crustaceans, and their waste is absorbed by microorganisms. They, in turn, are eaten by small crustaceans, which are eaten by fish. All this provides food for the waterbirds. Excretion and decay enrich the mud with nutrients to feed the mangroves, completing the cycle.

- More than one hundred species of marine life are found in Mangrove Cove. They range from marine worms to crustaceans, such as prawns and crabs.

Life's brimming with colours
Explore its myriad hues
Each one, so special

Lessons from Mother Nature

Reflection Time:

Lessons from Mother Nature

The clever dawn bird
Gets the bright, tasty fruits
Time for early starts

Lessons from Mother Nature

Reflection time:

Have there been times when you feel you have had an advantage in life or felt rewarded in some way because of being proactive or doing something earlier than others?

_____
_____
_____
_____
_____
_____
_____
_____
_____
_____
_____
_____
_____
_____
_____
_____
_____

When the time is right
I'll wear my favourite gowns
Time for a rest now

Lessons from Mother Nature

Reflection time:

I was walking along with my wife for our regular evening stroll. It was autumn, and the trees had let go of their leaves. My wife said to me, 'Isn't that great, trees let go of all their leaves when the time is right'? No questions asked, no fuss. Total trust in the universe.

Wait with patient love
You will see the cactus bloom
Cultivate patience

Lessons from Mother Nature

Did you know?

- The cactus plant, and in particular the yellow cactus flower, symbolises warmth, protection, and endurance.

- The cactus flower is a symbol of maternal love because it can endure and thrive in harsh conditions and, therefore, symbolic of a mother's unconditional love.

*Cooperation
And strong collaborations
A dream home is built*

Did you know:

- Ants are excellent architects - their nests are designed to provide just the right environment for larvae to grow. Some nests have a built-in ventilation system to circulate fresh air.

- An ant colony is like a factory. Nestmates work together to convert resources (food) into products. Different ants specialise on different jobs. The queen has the very specific role of laying eggs. Worker ants perform other duties, often depending on their age. Younger ants work inside the nest, taking care of the queen and her brood. Older workers go outside to gather food and defend the nest against enemies. Despite her size and royal title, the queen doesn't boss the workers around. Instead, workers decide which tasks to perform based on personal preferences, interactions with nestmates, and cues from the environment.

A dumped, old tyre
Can often be put to use
Create, improvise

Lessons from Mother Nature

Reflection time:

I had been once to a dump yard and found there an old, worn-out tyre. I found it a new home. I took it into my garden, coloured it red, rejuvenated it with red mud, and created new life in it by planting a cactus plant within it. I water it regularly, and it is now a centre of attraction in my lovely garden.

Sometimes magic is found outside the square, in places we least expect. Try to think outside the square and, laterally, go on roads less travelled and discover and rediscover the magic that abounds within and around you.

CPSIA information can be obtained
at www.ICGtesting.com
Printed in the USA
BVHW021922110819
555623BV00003B/18/P